# Shelley Holmes Ace Detective

MICHAELA MORGAN

Illustrated by Dee Shulman

DOGGYDINS

D0434522

OXFORD
UNIVERSITY PRESS

# OXFORD
## UNIVERSITY PRESS

Great Clarendon Street, Oxford OX2 6DP

Oxford University Press is a department of the University of Oxford.
It furthers the University's objective of excellence in research, scholarship,
and education by publishing worldwide in

Oxford   New York

Auckland   Cape Town   Dar es Salaam   Hong Kong   Karachi
Kuala Lumpur   Madrid   Melbourne   Mexico City   Nairobi
New Delhi   Shanghai   Taipei   Toronto

With offices in

Argentina   Austria   Brazil   Chile   Czech Republic   France   Greece
Guatemala   Hungary   Italy   Japan   Poland   Portugal   Singapore
South Korea   Switzerland   Thailand   Turkey   Ukraine   Vietnam

Oxford is a registered trade mark of Oxford University Press
in the UK and in certain other countries

First published 1998
This edition 2005

British Library Cataloguing in Publication Data
Data available

ISBN: 978-0-19-919975-4

5 7 9 10 8 6 4

Available in packs
Stage 12 More Stories A Pack of 6:
ISBN: 978-0-19-919971-6
Stage 12 More Stories A Class Pack:
ISBN: 978-0-19-919978-5
Guided Reading Cards also available:
ISBN: 978-0-19-919980-8

Cover artwork by Dee Schulman
Photograph of Michaela Morgan © Richard Drewe

Printed by Ashford Colour Press

# Chapter 1

It all started one day when
Shelley Holmes was a bit bored.

She was watching
the telly when
suddenly...

...she had a brilliant idea.

Shelley started to collect the things she needed.

Soon she had:

a pencil,

a notebook,

a detective hat,

and a detective office.

She also had a trusty assistant.

Shelley's best friend Kelly wasn't too keen on being the trusty assistant at first.

But in the end she agreed.

Dustbin was Shelley's dog.
He was called Dustbin for three reasons:
**1** The Rescue Home for Dogs had
found him (as a puppy) in a dustbin.

Shelley's family had taken him
home, looked after him and fed him.

**2** As he grew, he started to look more and more like a dustbin – round and fat and bulging.

ridges of metal

DUSTBIN

ridges of fat

DOG

**3** And he ate anything and everything.

SLURP   SLOBBER   CHOMP   MUNCH!

DOGGY DINS   DOGGY DINS   DOGGYDINS

He was a doggy dustbin.

# Chapter 2

Shelley Holmes (ace detective), Kelly (the trusty assistant), and Dustbin (the detective dog) had their first meeting in their new detective office (Shelley's bedroom).

They both thought
and thought
and thought.

They put their thinking caps on,
collected their thoughts,
racked their brains,
put their heads together,
daydreamed,
brooded
and worried.

But...

...it was a bit difficult to think with
all the noise Dustbin was making.

Dustbin was a very lively dog. He
was always up to something.

...he moment he was doing all of ...vourite things.

He was digging,

fighting,

barking and growling.

He was just about to start doing his most favourite thing of all – eating –

when Dad shouted: Shelley, will you keep that dog quiet!

Everyone liked to take their dogs to the canal.

Dustbin loved it. There were sticks to catch,

muddy puddles to roll in and...

...the canal to swim in.

Best of all, there were lots of other dogs to meet. There were dogs of all shapes and sizes. And all of them were friends with Dustbin.

There was Colin, the collie, and his owner.

Fifi, the poodle, and
her owner.

Spotty, the
dalmatian, and
his owner.

And Bully, the bulldog,
and his owner.

But a few of the others were missing.

'Hmm,' said Shelley. 'This could be our first mystery. What can have made these dogs like this?

'Come on, Dustbin, hurry up. Time to go home.'

# Chapter 3

Back in their detective office, Shelley and Kelly set to work.

'I read a story about dancing princesses once,' said Kelly. 'At night they'd sneak out of their palace, down a secret tunnel and go to a ball.

'The next morning they were all worn out and so were their shoes. Do you think these dogs could be up to something like that?'

'Perhaps they're just bored,' said Shelley.

'Or maybe they've been hypnotized,' said Kelly.

They were thinking so hard that at first, they didn't notice Dustbin.

He was fast asleep and snoring.

He didn't seem to want to wake up for anything. Not even his favourite food, Doggydins.

The next day Dustbin was still not his usual self.

He didn't want his toys.

He didn't want to be tickled.

And he was always falling asleep.

Always snoozing.

Always snoring.

Shelley and Kelly dragged Dustbin along to the vet's.

It wasn't easy.

It was very busy at the vet's.

'What did your dog eat yesterday?' the vet asked.

'Let me see...' said Shelley.
'Yesterday he ate
the TV Times,

a box of cornflakes,

(just the box, not the cornflakes)

a bunch of daffodils,

my dad's fishing bag,
and a pair of underpants.'

'Oh, that's not a lot for Dustbin,'
said Shelley. 'But what *is* odd is he
keeps falling asleep and he won't
touch his proper dog food. He used to
love Doggydins and now he won't
even look at it. It's very odd, very odd
indeed.'

Dustbin just nodded and continued
his doze.

'It's the same story with all these animals,' said the vet. 'They are all sick, off their food and sleepy. I don't know why.'

'It's a mystery,' sighed the vet.
'Yes, it is!' said Shelley.

# Chapter 4

Shelley and her trusty assistant got busy with their detective work. Dustbin wasn't much help.

| | |
|---|---|
| Shelley asked questions. | So did her trusty assistant. |
| Shelley collected evidence. | So did her trusty assistant. |

Dad tried to cheer them up. He even offered to take them fishing.

'A bit of fresh air will soon cheer you up,' he said. And off he went to find some fishing equipment for them.

Soon he was back with a big smile on his face and an enormous pile of stuff for Shelley and Kelly.

He had:
bits of equipment,

special clothes and spare dry socks

and a share of his maggots.

# Chapter 5

They took Dustbin with them in
the car.

But Dustbin snored all the way there.
He only woke up to nibble the car seat
a bit.

At the canal they all settled down
for a day's fishing.

Dad nearly caught a few.

WOBBLE

WOBBLE

Kelly … read a comic.

Shelley kept a look out for fish.

'That fish is not moving,' said Kelly.

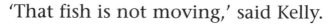

'It's flat out,' said Kelly.

'It's just lying there,' said Kelly.

After a while, they both realized –

Shelley and Kelly did not throw the dead fish back in the canal. Carefully, very carefully, without touching it, they put it in a plastic bag.

They noticed a few other things too.

And they made careful notes in their detective books. They even took some photos.

Then, they went back to Dad and Dustbin.

Dustbin had woken up briefly and eaten:

'I thought you said he'd gone off his food,' said Dad.

'He has, Dad. He still hasn't touched his Doggydins,' said Shelley.

Dustbin snoozed all the way home. He just woke once to burp.

# Chapter 6

Shelley and Kelly took the dead fish to the vet.

'Look,' they said.

'Even I can't cure a dead fish.'

'No, but you can look at it,' said Shelley. 'Why did it die and why is it a funny blue colour?'

'Of course we didn't touch it,' said Kelly, 'in case we caught something.'

'Disease,' Shelley explained. 'And we spotted some other things too. Look!'

She proudly showed their detective notebook and snaps.

'And the bird?' asked Kelly. 'What happened to that?'

'Easy peasy,' Shelley explained.

'Exactly,' said the vet.

'This could explain why all the other animals are sick. The water in the canal is polluted. If animals swim in it they will get ill. If they eat the poisoned fish or drink the water they could … die.'

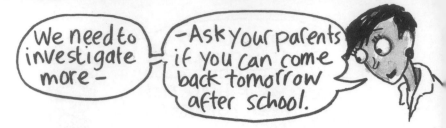

We need to investigate more –

– Ask your parents if you can come back tomorrow after school.

So the next day Shelley and Kelly set off with the vet. Dad came to help and brought Dustbin too.

'Then I can keep an eye on him,' he said.

They took samples of the water and then they all trailed up and down the canal bank looking for clues.

The vet found nothing much.

Dad found nothing much.

But Dustbin found ... absolutely nothing. He was asleep most of the time.

zzzzz

And all Kelly and Shelley found was...

But it was niffy, whiffy, strong and pongy and absolutely DISGUSTING.

Dustbin woke up briefly and sniffed the air. Bad smells were what he liked best.

**Don't you dare, Dustbin!**

*pongy whiff!*

Before Shelley could stop him, he'd jumped in the water and was swimming to the other side.

He started digging into the canal bank.

'What is that dog doing?' sighed Dad. And then he saw.

**He's found a pipe hidden by weeds!**

Out of the pipe came frothy bubbles, slightly blue and powerfully pongy.

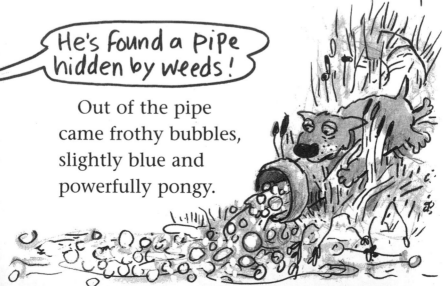

'That's it!' said the vet.

That's what's poisoning the water.

Call the Police!

Dad shouted.

Call the army!

Kelly shouted.

'We'll call the Health Inspector. That should do it!' said the vet. 'Then we'll find out where it's coming from and we'll –'

And then she stopped.

'Oh, Shelley!' she said.

Your dog!

Dustbin had fallen to the ground. He was panting, trying to catch his breath and twitching.

'Dustbin!' Shelley shouted.

But Dustbin just raised his head and gazed at her. Then he gave a little sigh, closed his eyes and slumped. He lay perfectly still.

# Chapter 7

Kelly got ready to dive in.
'NO!' said the vet.

> That water's not fit to swim in. You'd get as sick as Dustbin.

Dad borrowed a boat and soon he had Dustbin back on the bank.
The vet sighed.

> It doesn't look good. Get my bag! Quick!

She forced some nasty purple stuff into Dustbin's mouth.

Dustbin was very, very sick.
They raced Dustbin back to her office.
'I'll keep him here,' the vet said.

> I'll do my best for him.

The next few days were crazy days.
Men in white suits came and tracked
the pipe back to a factory.

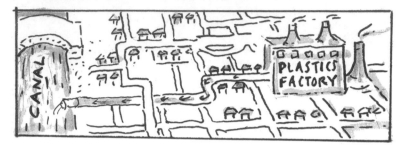

It was in
the newspapers.

It was on
the telly.

But Shelley and Kelly couldn't get
excited about it. They were too
worried about Dustbin.

The vet had shaken her head. 'He swallowed a large dose of the poison straight from the pipe,' she said.

'But I gave him medicine straight away which gives him some chance.

Now all we can do is wait and see.

| So they waited... | ...and waited... |
| ...and waited... | ...and what did they see? |

'Luckily your dog seems to have a strong stomach,' said the vet.

'It's a cast iron stomach,' Shelley said.

'Woof!' said Dustbin.

So the pollution was stopped. The factory cleaned up its act. The canal and fish were saved. Some local people cleaned up the canal.

But best of all, Dustbin was saved.

And he cleaned out his doggy bowl right down to the last lick.

He also ate:

a recipe book,

a box of tissues,
(the box and the tissues)

one of Dad's
fishing boots,

Just a bit of it...

a bunch of tulips,

a wastepaper basket,

more Doggydins,

and Dad's
dinner too.

'OY, that dog!' shouted Dad.
But he didn't really mind.

'Everything has turned out fine,' said Shelley.

So off they went, with Dustbin as their detective dog, to find one.

# *About the author*

My favourite character in this story is Dustbin the dog. I had a dog like him once. Mine attacked the phone, chewed it and then buried it in the garden.

Shelley is a bit like me. I always liked pretending to be the heroes of books and television programmes. Unfortunately I was never able to persuade anyone to be my trusty assistant. The good thing about writing stories is that you can put bits of real life in them and then you can go wild imagining things.